Dan's first collection of poetry is Applied Mathematics, published by Burning Eye. Laureate, he has been Poet National Trust Stowe, and C had pieces commissioned and the Beaney Library. Da including Glastonbury Festi Sofar Sounds Auckland, Edi

Dan creates pioneering work using crowdsourced and outdoor poetry for organisations such as the Royal Academy of Arts, National Museum of Scotland, and the European Commission. He is an experienced project manager, coordinating literature and performance programmes for arts organisations. He co-produces and hosts poetry versus comedy gig Stand Up & Slam, and worst-poet-wins spectacle The Anti-Slam. Often working in scientific contexts, Dan has appeared at popular science shows and talks - and is half of Dr. Illingworth and Mr. Simpson, devising interdisciplinary science communication events and projects.

As an experienced educator, Dan is an enthusiastic, insightful, and adaptable workshop leader. He convenes and lectures on the 'Writing for the Spoken Word' module at Canterbury Christ Church University, and delivers primary and secondary school classes around the U.K. - including work for First Story, Barbican Centre, and Apples and Snakes. He also runs both creative writing and professional development sessions for adults.

www.dansimpsonpoet.co.uk

@dansimpsonpoet

DAN SIMPSON
Totally Cultured

Burning Eye

Copyright © 2019 Dan Simpson

The author asserts the moral right under the Copyright, Designs and Patents Act 1988 to be identified as the author of this work.

All rights reserved. No part of this publication may be reproduced, stored in a retrieval system, or transmitted, in any form or by any means without the prior written consent of the author, nor be otherwise circulated in any form of binding or cover other than that in which it is published and without a similar condition being imposed on the subsequent purchaser.

This edition published by Burning Eye Books 2019

www.burningeye.co.uk

@burningeyebooks

Burning Eye Books
15 West Hill, Portishead, BS20 6LG

ISBN 978-1-911570-28-8

Totally Cultured

*To my creative partners
Lucy, Paula, and Sam:
my good friends.*

*This poetry business
can be a lonely place
but you make it so much more
companionable.*

Thank you.

CONTENTS

They Should Have Sent a Poet	11
In These Days	14
A Poet's Debt	16
Sacrifice	17
Dad's Black Cab	20
New Music Review, 1985	22
Learning Your Name	23
3.57pm on the Last Day of School at Bexleyheath Clock Tower	24
Stairs	25
Nostalgia	26
Bookology	28
Limericku	29
Poem Written Whilst on Hold to a Call Centre	30
Obsidian Images	32
Oh Wow Country	34
Dress Code	36
Packing a Poem	37
Hangover	39
Breaking	41
This Be Just the Verse to Say	42
A Super Powerful Haiku	43
Metadata	44
An Email I Received	46
OkCupid	50
Negotiation	51
Love Drunk	52
My Mistress's Eyes	54
Totally Cultured	55
Saturday/Sunday	60
Not Cricket	61
Christmas Office Exit Strategy	64
A Shape Poem	66

THEY SHOULD HAVE SENT A POET

'No words to describe it. Poetry! They should have sent a poet.'

Dr Ellie Arroway, Contact

So they did:
they actually sent a poet
into outer space.

Her mission:
describe the indescribable.
Easy.

She took it in stride, at first.
After all, she was a professional
had wrestled with the unknowable
fleeting feelings of heart and mind
made the internal understandable
reflected on the world
on nature and humanity
even penned a couple of pieces about stars in her time:
she was qualified, if anyone ever was
to be the first poet in space.

The press went for the story in a big way –
Where No Poet Has Gone Before (*Mirror*)
Space: the Final Sonneteer (*Times*)
Star Poet to Explore the Uni-Verse (*Sun*)
Dark Matter… of the Soul (*Guardian*).

The Mission Commander was less impressed:
'I don't care how many Pulitzers you've won'
(none)
'or how many Nobel Prizes for Literature'
(zip);
'you're taking the place of someone
who could actually be useful
and you're here to write'
– they almost spat the word –
'poetry.'

Words… no words
would come to the poet at first
all far too beautiful
to be captured in verse
trapped in imprecise imagery.

What form, what simile
could do justice to the violent grandeur of a collapsing star?
The awesome subtlety of a supernova?
The marbled depths of a nebula?
Or paintbrush-stroke galaxies orbiting one another?

Talk about writers' block:
despite the zero-G atmosphere
she was crushed by the gravity of the situation.

She lurked in her cabin for days
almost paralysed with fear
whilst her crewmates went about their business
like they knew what they were doing
which, of course, they did.

She slept, mostly
to avoid the responsibility
that comes with being
a poet.

She wakes to an alarm
clanging like a writer dropping cliché after cliché
blaring into her head like an off-key juxtaposition
her sleep an inappropriate metaphor
for the air onomatopoeically escaping her room.

Running down the corridor
she is fear personified
feet beating a skittish rhythm
her thoughts all broken lines
an enjambment of anxiety.

She rhymes her keycard with the bridge's access pad:
bodies slumped like an understatement
repeated assonance shapes
twisted consonance angles.

Looking down at the console
red lights flashing
she sighs, and says:

'They should have sent an astronaut.'

IN THESE DAYS

In these
status-updating no-time-for-waiting
days.

In these
deep-faking Internet-breaking
chatbot-talking monitor-gawking
days.

In these
Bluetooth-enabled high-speed-cabled
iPod-shuffling Uber-summoning
headphone-wearing Turing-testing
robot-rising targeted-advertising
days.

In these
Twitter-trolling inaccurate-polling
podcast-rambling celebrity-cancelling
illegal-downloading AI-coding
emoji-using journalist-abusing
hot-take-writing social-media-fighting
data-mining left-right-swiping
virtue-signalling online-petitioning
iCloud-leaking firewall-breaching
days.

In these
expert-doubting ALL-CAPS-SHOUTING
password-leaking live-Twitch-streaming
Spotify-listening WhatsApp-pinging
3D-printing Netflix-chilling
Facebook-friending GIF-sending
email-spamming forum-banning
cars-self-driving ask-hiveminding
always-browsing fake-news-shouting
sponsored-posting Tinder-ghosting
days.

Days
of CCTV and the on-demand economy
of viral memes and learning machines
of cyber warfare and rogue spyware
of post-truth politics and pay-per-clicks
of click factories and always-drained batteries
of voicemail hacking and iPhone tracking
of microtransactions and screen distractions
of political clicktivism and pics of kittens
of clickbait headlines and GDPR fines
of 'Hey, Siri'-ing and #everything.

I sometimes
stop.

Stop.

Stop.

I turn off my computer
I put down my phone
I go out into the wilderness
breathe the fresh mountain air deeply
let spring water trickle through my fingers
feel the sun's warmth against my upturned face
the thick grasses of the plains tickling my bare toes.

I close my eyes
listen for the gentle sounds of nature
I sigh, and think:

I should post this on Instagram.

A POET'S DEBT

'You're behind this month
by two heavy sighs
and one contemplative reverie'
the Emotional Impact Manager
for NatWest says.

'We couldn't possibly approve
your application for an extended metaphor
at this time
or, indeed, at this rhyme.'

The poet nods, understanding
tries a small smile
promises to make it up next month
walks home
heart beating an irregular metre.

SACRIFICE

It's just a little sacrifice!
We're not asking much.
Just don't go out for brunch
and eat smashed avocado on sourdough
all the time.
That's all.

Maybe stop spending all that money on flat whites.
Perhaps cycle, instead of getting the Tube?
Don't buy books!
Borrow them from the library
(if your local library still exists).

Here's one: share a Netflix login with friends!
Forget festivals.
Forget the cinema.
Forget a new smartphone
trainers
jacket
bag
jeans
dress.

Don't eat out.
Don't go travelling.
Don't go to university:
£9,000 a year plus living expenses?
Not. Worth. It.
Get a job
with opportunities for promotion.

But if you must go to university
because you have 'aspirations' or 'dreams':
study something vocational.
Be practical.
Live at home.
Hope your parents don't mind that you're taking up space.
Don't mind that you're still taking up space.

Don't go on joyful nights out
or have experiences that will change you
and your attitudes for the better.
No takeaways.
No nightclubs.
No friends, ideally.
No temptation to have a swift one after finals.

Graduate as soon as possible.
Master's? No.
PhD? Please.
Find a well-paying job immediately –
there are loads of those going around.

If you have to, go into one of those highly sought-after
glamorous unpaid internships –
after all, 'experience' can put food in your mouth
and gladness in your heart
far better than a fair wage for a fair job.

Get that job
and save 90% of your income
after necessary expenses.
Necessary expenses do not include:
a gym membership
a car
decent toilet paper
buying sandwiches for lunch
(make your own sandwiches, you profligate)
restaurants nicer than Nando's
(you can go for a Nando's; I'm not a monster).

Do not treat yourself
to a glass of wine on a Tuesday evening
because bloody hell you are exhausted and stressed
and your boss is awful
and your single bedroom
in your five-person flatshare
an hour and a half from where you work
is the only space you can call your own
and even though rent is 50% of your laughable salary

you're grateful for that
and want to treat yourself
to a cheeky glass of Rioja.

Dating is completely unnecessary.
Meet the right person for you before you're twenty-two.
Make sure they have the same attitude to saving.
Cohabit a room barely big enough for one.
Split the extortionate rent in two.
Pool your resources
choose a shoebox house you'll live on top of each other in
that is your dream home now.

Don't.
Break.
Up.
Break-ups are expensive.

Be stronger.
Take the pressure.
You can do this.
You can do this.
You can do this.
You are compressed carbon becoming diamond
hardened to the outside world
ready to save yourself
in a house of your own making.

Work harder.
Save more.
Give up your twenties to your savings account.
Give up your thirties to your savings account.
Slaughter yourself.
Let blood.

It's just a little sacrifice.

DAD'S BLACK CAB

Dad's a black cab man:
grafts hard all day
all warm chat and charm
a canny bard that gladly attacks cab ranks.

All want a cab:
smart bar staff
sparkly gymnasts
daft granddads
brassy grandmas
sarky Yanks: 'Blah blah blah'
larky stags: 'Lads lads lads!'

A hand sharply flags
flat palm prays skywards
a brash man calls hymnals:
'Halt! Cab!'
Dad parks:
'Ahha! Canary Wharf.'

Dad's a pathway analyst
starts a sly atlas maths
charts all maps
tracks back many yards:
gnarls at St Pancras
bypass Pall Mall and Strand
flyby Aldwych and Bank
anarchy at Trafalgar, V&A, RADA...

Data-rhythms sync, standby: a plan
Dad says, 'Away!'

Dad plays a part
talks backwards, chatty.
'Shhhh!' says man, angry
as hand taps at smartpad
snarls at call alarm, blasts talk back –
'What an ass'
Dad says, dryly.

Dad plays Adam Ant, ABBA
A-Ha, AC/DC
Alt-J, Frank Zappa, Alabama 3
as cars blast past.

Abracadabra: cab parks at Canary Wharf.
'A grand,' Dad says – a gag.
Man says, 'Nah,' at that
can't pay – ran away!
'Crafty bastard!' Dad gasps
and 'grrrs' – a black cab hazard.

Dad adapts
day crawls past…
and dark.

Back at flat
Dad yawns
warm snacks
TV, a G&T
and – at last –
Dad naps.

NEW MUSIC REVIEW, 1985

written using words that first entered the dictionary in 1985

Boyband supercell Dead Cat Bounce are total trendoids
the go-to alternative-pop multi-tools
of brain-dump biodiversity.

Their song 'Elephant in the Room'
the bunker-busting title track
from their second album Attachment Parenting
features drag-and-drop breakbeat samples
layered over lead singer and compositionist Bucky Ball's
double-double-quick Old Occitan beatboxing.

Dealing with 24/7 caller-ID screening
by a Vietnamese potbellied pig
the song is perfect for both ciabatta-eating parents
sipping lattes at their step aerobics classes
and the band's codependent, cosmeceutically
elm yellow French-tipped teen fans.

Here's the 411:
an FX-heavy music video
featuring anime babes in tankinis
drinking microbrews in a crack house
may overwhelm synesthetes
but does nothing to their cleantech image –
a quantum dot in the ocean
serving as steganographic adware
of baby-monitored, wholesome goodness.

A recent bum-rush for tickets
knocked down stockade fences
demonstrating that –
at least for this carbon-copied
graphene-deep, "cool beans" band –
the strong anthropic principle is alive and well.

Rating:
C++.

LEARNING YOUR NAME

Remember learning your alphabet?

The smell of pencils freshly sharpened
in the classroom of your infant school
those potato-stamp poster paintings on the wall
and the plastic stickiness of PVA glue
rubbed onto chubby fingertips.

Peeled off in skin-thin fingerprints
as you tried to stick the pieces of yourself together
a picture made of sugar-paper cut-out shapes
all imprecise and clumsy
rough and bumpy around the edges.

Like the letters you tried to write
in heavy-handed crayon or bright felt-tip pens
gripped tight in balled-up fists
as you sounded out the syllables of yourself
spelled out on a tag hung on a coat peg.

The lines and curls of you not fully knowable, yet
but you would grow to claim it
make it your own
be able to say, with pride:

'Hello.
My name is...'

3.57PM ON THE LAST DAY OF SCHOOL AT BEXLEYHEATH CLOCK TOWER

      By the clock tower bus station
school leavers are waiting
blazing with anticipation
    blazers slung over shoulders
emblazoned bags and work folders
    lazily flung
           to the
                floor.

Ties no longer knotted
    not top-notch
a botched job
      peanutted
shirts half stuck in trousers
    half untucked.

Boys:
    dumbstruck
        by blouses
girls' skirts given short shrift
    shifted up
    by inches
    over hours
rules forever flouted.

A golden moment ignites
    amazing and bright
        the temperature raised
they're brazen
    emboldened by sunlight
controlled fight or flight
    holding such life:

they move on.

STAIRS

The staircase in my house plays music
every time I descend it
my feet half-turned sideways
on narrow piano keys
bouncing down quickly
almost only toes tapping
each step.

I know the creaks intimately
the springing-back of wood under carpet
a series of muddled notes
that fall and rise with each step.

I practise my scales now
bringing twenty-odd years of possessions
up and down
listening to the silences between footfalls.

They are filled with more than can ever be said
by the making of music.

NOSTALGIA

Do you remember nostalgia?

Ah, I remember remembering:
back in the day
when we thought back
to days gone by
and said, 'Those were the days'
and they really were –
the days, that is.

Those good old days
when we talked about the past
like a domestic country
everything knowable
and easy
when reminiscing was a simple pleasure
unlike now.

When the kids didn't know they were born
because they weren't, yet
but even that was a joy to contemplate:
sepia-toned memories of memories
were easy to come by
everyone happy remembering
all of the time.

Sentimental about nostalgia?
Me?
Hardly.
Listen: let me tell you
about a better era
of pining for the past.

I remember it as if it was yesterday
because it was yesterday
and the day before that
stretching back into all the yesterdays of last week
all the last weeks of last month
all the last months of last year
the last years of the entirety of our lives
the entire lives of generations gone by.
I remember them all.

What simple times they were, I seem to recall
when walking down memory lane was easy.
Now I stumble on every little remembrance
longing for that bygone age of classic wistfulness.

But I do wish we could turn the clock back
even by a few minutes – seconds, even
but alas
I remember nostalgia:
it's not what it used to be.

BOOKOLOGY

The books are flying off the library shelves again
literally.

With a soft crack and shudder of pages
translucent wings unfurl from their spines
rice-paper thin, they look fragile
but are more than enough to lift
even the weightiest tome.

Flittering around the fluorescent lights
quietly buzzing with half-heard stories
the books swoop and nose-dive
playfully chase children around the stacks
dropping bookmarks absolutely everywhere
but no one minds: 'They eat boredom'
someone – probably a librarian – reminds us.

Each book is gently caught and calmed
any corners found folded are straightened out
efficiently stamped and details recorded
territory and habits noted down
before being released back into the wild
as if it is a species threatened with extinction
(though everyone knows
books are incredibly common in the world).

As the evening darkens, the books return to roost
nesting on shelves and tables, in bags and drawers
some lucky enough to find a large pocket to sleep in.

The books tuck in their wings
shake the dust from their jackets
and curl up with one another.

LIMERICKU

Once a man Mike, who
liked to write quick limericks
hidden in haiku.

POEM WRITTEN WHILST ON HOLD TO A CALL CENTRE

Thank you for calling this premium-rate number
for a service you're already paying for.

Please select from the following options
so we can better redirect your call
through a labyrinthine series
of increasingly vague descriptions.

Press 1 if you have some sort of problem, issue, or difficulty.
Press 2 if you're experiencing something right now.
Press 3 to speak to a badly-trained temp who knows less about
                                            the product than you do.

Press 4 or this call will be terminated.
Press 5 to return to the previous menu – which doesn't exist.
DO NOT PRESS 9 UNDER ANY CIRCUMSTANCES.
Press your forehead to the table to signify a general sense of
                                                          ennui.

Remember: your call is important to us
in a sort of detached, abstract way
like one might care about the minor illness of a distant relative.

Thank you for holding
we will answer your call
as soon as financially prudent.

In the meantime, enjoy this repetitive musical interlude
which is a synth cover of the first thirty seconds
of a popular song from a number of years ago
on infinite repeat.

You are currently being held
in what we laughingly refer to as a 'queue'
but is really more of a mosh-pit clusterfuck
of increasingly irate customers.

Our classically trained voiceover actor
is pre-emptively sorry for the inevitable delay
which we foresaw but did nothing about
and his somewhat ingratiatingly sincere tone
has been designed to further incense you.

All of our operators are currently busy
by which we mean we have significantly underfunded
our customer service centres
and we must apologise for the slowness of our system
but unfortunately all of our systems
are all of our systems today.

DO NOT SAY THE WORD 'KAFKAESQUE'
or your call will be terminated.

Congratulations: you are now first in the queue
and we are ready to forward your call
to the next section of the telephone queuing system.

Thank you for calling.
Fuck off.

OBSIDIAN IMAGES

Take your block of polished obsidian
hold it up to the sky
as an offering to the social media gods
their algorithms unknowable
as mystical and arcane as numerology.

Mutter Kabbalistic sequences
like a catechism
as if you know how to decipher prophecy
in the tarot cards of data:
twenty-four likes
seventy-three retweets
one hundred and eleven impressions
six hundred and forty-eight followers
over four thousand fans.

Digital soothsayer:
scatter status updates like bones
throw up dust into the cloud
where it will last forever
or, at least, until the servers go down.

Look deeply with your third eye
phone in the results
from any sign you can draw meaning from
read whatever you can in the patterns.

Sceptics may disregard metrics
but you know better:
your engagement with the hidden world
of sacred algorithmic geometry is increasing.

Open yourself to mind-altering experiences:
skin up with a layer of paper-thin confidence
wrapped around smoke and mirrors
breathe deep the hashtags of consequence
filters applied to mediate some substance
from the resinous moment of exposure.

Take a good, hard look at your selfie
in this black mirror
the pose you struck, dumb
no words: you are a statue
flawed and flawless
toppling, your face fractures
cracks from where you dropped yourself
wishing you were encased in something more resilient
than flesh.

OH WOW COUNTRY

Dear New Zealand:
as I, poet, travelled around you
feet tracing a path from north to south
there and back again
eyes roaming over your peaks and plains
people said I'd be inspired by you.

But I'll be honest with you, New Zealand:
it's a bit much.

You started as an 'Oh wow' country
each place I stopped
stopping me in my tracks
a loud 'Oh, wow'
escaping my lips
as I took in your natural splendour
again
and again
and again.

In isolation any one of these views would be incredible
but with so many at every turn
each 'Oh, wow' became quieter
each awe-inducing vista
more run-of-the-mill.

Oh, look!
Yet another scenic lake:
deep blues and sparkling turquoise the colour of life itself
set against a ruggedly handsome mountain range
of darkly alluring rock picked out in touches of white
a riot of trees patchwork green rushing downhill
the sky the colour skies are in children's books
all vibrant brush strokes of literally heaven.

Enough already:
you're basically just showing off
my eyes actually hurt from all this beauty
it's too much
like #nofilter was made for you.

On this, our first date
I feel underdressed
embarrassed in your radiant presence
you in your fanciest, most elegant clothes
your finest, timeless jewellery
a perfectly coiffed haircut
your eyebrows totally on fleek
without seeming to make any effort at all.
How do you do it, New Zealand?

I mean, even your trees are ridiculous:
pohutukawa are dressed for Christmas all year
manuka are arboreal superheroes
and with silver ferns you're really gilding the lily.

New Zealand, you're not simply breathtaking;
you're making me hyperventilate
as each new picturesque landscape
reveals yet another pinnacle of aesthetic pleasure.

Please pass me the brown paper bag
of mediocre English countryside
just so I can catch my breath –
I don't want to be so dizzy
when I come back to appreciate you
the next time.

DRESS CODE

Flip-flops
    and a tuxedo
does not mean
    smart casual.

PACKING A POEM

It begins neatly:
words laid out carefully
similar items sitting in small piles
ready to be placed in an appropriate spot.

Make use of all available space:
tuck verbs into nouns
like squashing socks into shoes.

Economy: that's what we're after –
no waste.

Fold the lines once
twice
halve their length
again
don't worry about the creases for now
fit them down the sides of the poem
some extra padding around the edges
protecting the meaning in the middle.

Roll verses into one another
make them multi-layered and dense
a complication of essentials
like towels and trousers
wrapped around toothbrushes.

Take your time.
You're doing well.

Then suddenly
give in to frustration
or laziness
that deadline approaches
and you just have to leave ASAP.

Give up on your method and let your packing run wild
piling anything in anywhere it seems to fit
mixing metaphors with un-ironed shirts –
even a few crumpled clichés have snuck their way in
hidden amongst the private toiletries and assorted devices.

Don't worry:
stuff bras and pants in the gaps
since everyone likes a good underwear joke.

Leave extraneous material hanging out the sides
barely understandable bits of words
that squeeze out
when you eventually go to close the lid.

Which won't shut, of course
so you sit on your poem to close it
pull the zips hard
catching letters between teeth and slider
hearing the crack of the poem's spine under your weight.

It'll probably be fine:
you can pick up anything you've forgotten later
in performance.

I mean, who has the time, really
to properly pack a poem?

HANGOVER

Glottal snore
throat raw
bad head
bedhead

dry mouth
brain sore
hangdog
dog breath

short leash
short fuse
damp dribble
seeing double
face grizzle
old stubble

feeling that I am in trouble...

Down local
quiet one
be social
come home

plan fails
derails
details:
one pint, two pint, three pint, four...
five pint, six pint, seven pint... more?

Stomach churn
eyes burn
thoughts whirl
that girl?

Blank space
black eye
bright light
some guy

gutter mouth
gutter ball
big bloke
brick wall
red mist
really pissed.

Really pissed
clenched fist
clenched teeth
blood rush
room spin
sawdust.

Bar club
walk cab
stop, buy
best kebab
chips, Coke
girl's phone…

How the hell did I get home?

BREAKING

a Golden Shovel, after Jennifer Maiden

Suddenly, I felt old:
a night watching the hollowing out of Europe.

The TV looked at me; I just stared –
the calm surface of pundits' faces at
last broke like waves against coastal barriers. Her
tired eyes lost in mine over breakfast
the right bread buttered
as she put together her
things for another day of work, grabbing a croissant
on the way out; as she sipped
a glass of orange juice, I put on the coffee.

Italian roast gurgling into the pot which
always left a burn mark and tasted
bittersweet, like
the way things always are, a
kiss goodbye, and the door shut: a fired gun.

THIS BE JUST THE VERSE TO SAY

with apologies to Philip Larkin and William Carlos Williams

They eat your plums, your mum and dad
they may not mean to but they do
fill iceboxes with faults they had
and ate some breakfast: a 'fuck you'.

Their plums were eaten in their turn
by fools who left old-style notes
who, probably, half soppy-stern
had delicious plums in their throats.

Man hands on iceboxes to man
so sweet, so cold; a coastal shelf
forgive as early as you can
and don't save any plums yourself.

A SUPER POWERFUL HAIKU

The subject matter
of this meaningful haiku:
TBD.

METADATA

The title of this poem
is not the poem.
Your name
is not you.

You can read into titles
interpret and analyse
but metadata can only tell us so much.

There are many ways to describe a poem
or a person
but none will make you feel much of anything
about anything:
only the poem – or person – can do that
hopefully.

The workings of words cannot be easily captured.
I can record metadata:
this poem was started on 10 July 2016
there are twelve stanzas in this poem
the author is Dan Simpson (hi)
it was written on a MacBook
it's about metadata and humanity
it starts like this – quite meta, some data –
and builds to something about humanity.

None of these things are the poem.

Here is a way of describing you:
your heart is approximately 12cm long
9cm wide, 6cm deep
weighs about 300 grams
will beat 2.5 billion times in your lifetime.

Metadata:
none of it tells us what your heart contains
the light and heaviness it will create
what each beat will mean to someone else.

Here is the poem:
metadata can draw an outline
but it can't fill in the details –
you are too subtle for statistical analysis
too intangible to have your output parsed:
you are more than your descriptors
too beautiful to have truth found in facts.

We are too often reduced
to simple numbers and demographic keywords
plugged into algorithms and assumptions
that cannot truly appreciate us.

We relate: take our pattern-seeking brains
and put them to work
to focus our brilliance on the shadows
that darken us in despairing moments
to love the brightness of our spectrum selves
the glorious electromagnetic radiance of living.

So forget metadata –
we are raw, unprocessed data itself
outliers beyond the predictions of probability
streaming live and electric into the world.

We contain such quantities of delicate information
so many multitudes of subtle meanings
that no software will ever understand us
but we can, at least, try
to understand one another.

AN EMAIL I RECEIVED

Hi Dan,

Hope you're well. Are you well? I do hope you're well.
How's the family? Wife and kids? Do you have those?
I can't remember, since we only occasionally email
for purely professional reasons
but you can't email in purely business language
since it seems impolite and blunt
and I'd hate to come off like that.
I'M A GOOD PERSON, honestly –
please don't judge me by my emails!

Anyway, I hope you're well. Are you? Keeping busy?
Snowed under? I know how that feels!
But it's good to be busy, isn't it?
That's what we say.
So best to pretend we're both really super busy
and have no time
to write long emails going into every little detail
about ourselves.

Thank you for asking if I was well in your last email.

I am well, thank you.
Mostly well.
A little under the weather!
Aren't we all?
All that work I'm snowed under
no wonder I'm a little run-down
but I'm well
apart from that
mostly well
better when I'm not in the office.
Typical!

Anyway, I hope you're well.
Busy though, I imagine!
Super busy.
Lots of emails to deal with!
I know how that goes.

I dream of a day when I've answered all my emails
when I can loosen my tie
leave the office
roam and ramble
in a Wi-Fi-free part of the world…

But anyway
I do hope you're well.
Are you well? Do tell.
Do you have an inner life?
A mind of your own?
I think you must
and I want to acknowledge your personhood
your sense of being an emotional and complete individual
with hopes and dreams
and maybe a dog?

Do you have a dog?

I hope your dog is well.
I really don't want to depersonalise you in this email.
It's so impersonal, isn't it?
Email?
What do you think?
Please do tell me at length your thoughts –
we'll get round to dealing
with those professional matters later

on a morning when the sunrise heralds more than another day
   of emails
the early rays of light warming your naked flesh
the bright beams firing up your refreshed mind
and you can breathe, slowly, ready to encounter the world
this world of wonder and brilliance.

Anyway, I hope you're well!
Happy Christmas/Easter/holidays/New Year/birthday as
 appropriate.
What did you get up to?
Something nice, I hope.
It's always nice to see the family.
Have some downtime.
Get away from the desk.
The desk of perpetual confinement, I call it!

Not literally, of course.
I'm not actually tied with thick rope to my wheelie chair
hands forever bound to a keyboard
attention monitored by bespoke eye-tracking software
definitely not that.
It's more a prison for the mind
am I right?

But anyway.
Hope you're well!
I'm just emailing to say hello, really
and that I hope you're well.

Forget about anything business-related.
We'll get round to that in another email.
Perhaps you could email me later today?
I do so enjoy getting emails from you
even though they're purposeful and to the point –
it gives me such a glimpse of the outside world.

I can almost smell the honeysuckle of your garden
mingling with the scent of fresh bread from your kitchen
see your wife beckoning me in for dinner
feel the embrace of your children
who know nothing about email
and are perfectly content with an all-encompassing hug
and a bedtime story.

Anyway, do drop me an email back when you get the chance.
I know you're busy
what with all the emails
but I hope you're well apart from that.
Are you well? I'm sure you are.

Please find nothing attached to this email
and expect another email in a few days
where I'll forget the attachment again
and don't worry that this message is marked as urgent
flagged for your immediate attention.

There's no real reason for that, in all honesty.
It's definitely not a call for help
a desperate message sent from the darkness
where they are always watching me
it's not urgent at all
since if it was important
I would have phoned
and not emailed.

No one actually speaks any more, do they?
Anyway, I hope you're well.

All the best
hope you're well
XXXXX XXXXXXXXXX

OKCUPID

A bar
a boy
a girl
quite coy.

We smiled
we talked
we laughed
we walked.

Her home
alone
we kissed
undressed.

Her phone
it rang
the voice
a man.

Her bro?
Oh no!

I had
to go
climb out
window.

No luck
no chance
no socks
no pants.

My fault
I know
I was
stupid:
      never use
      OkCupid.

NEGOTIATION

We don't talk any more.

Instead, we negotiate
a little give and take
to maintain peace:
a ceasefire barely adhered to.

A dialogue is called for
an accord must be found
so we pose for photos
broad friendly smiles
warmly clasped hands
a look down the camera:
we mean business.

Bringing our grievances to the table
it's all laid out
positions defended
allegations made
the past revisited –
we turn from a delicate dance of diplomacy
to emotionally charged ideology.

You take an unreasonable stance
accusing me of the same
until finally it's time
for plain speaking.

I say 'pizza'
you say 'curry'
followed by a lengthy silence.

LOVE DRUNK

Drunk and stumbling
they fall into Love
spilling Love's lager
all down his shirt.

'Sorry, mate'
one of them starts to say
but Love is having none of it
because although Love is a mean drunk
he's meaner when he's sober –
and that was his first drink
after a very
long
day.

Love is sick of these kids
who can't handle themselves
falling into him
constantly
clumsy feet treading on his toes
all-elbow embraces poking him in the ribs
leaning-in heads resting on his shoulder.

Love is not that adorable cherub any more:
he's grizzled and world-weary
deep battle-line creases in his face
heart tarnished and blackened –
a tough old bastard
with the scars to prove it.

So tonight
Love is here to drink beer
and break hearts
and now Love
is all out of beer.

Love turns to the couple
smiles without warmth
says, 'Don't *mate* me, mate'
and throws the first punch.

MY MISTRESS'S EYES

My mistress's eyes are exactly like the sun:
thermonuclear fusion reactions
between hydrogen and helium
taking place at their core

which makes buying sunglasses
somewhat of a problem.

TOTALLY CULTURED

Tonight's a big one, lads
let's get totally and utterly cultured
completely off-our-faces wrecked
on art and the finest things.

Oi oi! Pre-drinks at mine!
Dust off that red I've been saving
since 1969 – a good vintage
for the Châteauneuf-du-Pape –
pour the wine, mate
time to get on the lash.

Sip it.
Sip it!
SIP IT!
Savour the burst of ripening cherries
enjoy that long oak finish
the notes of vanilla and elderflower coming through.
Wicked.

Wahey!
Giles is here, finally
absolute party animal
always up for a rave
brings the dirtiest beats
what absolute filth have you brought, Giles?

Shostakovich's Fourth
by the Vienna Philharmonic
ON VINYL?
Fucking hell, mate
what a banger.
Put. It. On. Now.
Choooon!

Lads: we need to get going
my chauffeur's pulled the Bentley round
time to get on the banter train
if we're going to make our dinner reservations.
I thought we'd have a cheeky
Hélène Darroze at the Connaught
only two Michelin stars, lads
but it'll do for lining the stomach.

Here we go – don't forget your cummerbund, Giles
you absolute ledge
the Archbishop of Banterbury there
really putting the semi-
into semi-formal.

Aw, come on, mate, don't take offence
we're just having a laugh
it's just a bit of banter
chill out, yeah?

Here we are, lads!
Time to get our munch on.
Beluga caviar to start?
Why not, lads?
It's a big one, after all!
And I'll have the pheasant for main
the La Madeline au Truffe to finish.
Proper.

Giles! Peaking a bit early, mate?
You can't even finish your sherry?
See it away, son.
You're totally mental!
But lads – eat up –
time to hit up Sadler's Wells.

It's only a short walk
but I don't want to miss the orchestra warming up
bunch of legends.

That moment of potential coming together
the inner workings of a great human machine
applying skill to artistry
the endeavour of humanity to create more
to transcend the individual for the group
community embodied in the fading strains
of woodwind and brass, string and percussion
that magical instance of life itself flowing through
telling us that nature is not to be feared, but embraced…

Oh, God, Giles has been sick.
Too much pre-canapé action for him
he's a 24-carat liability, a right mess
phone his wife to pick him up –
you're going home in a Land Rover!

Anyway, lads, let's not let it spoil our evening!
Let's make it off the chain
for Giles, yeah?
Let's get absolutely battered by culture!

It's coming home!
It's coming home!
It's coming:
ballet's coming home.

Here we are, lads, Sadler's Wells
breathe it in, lads
take in that atmosphere
it's absolutely going off up in here!

Where are our seats?
Are these our seats?
Those people are sitting in our seats.
I won't stand for that.
No, mate.
It's well disrespectful.
We always sit there.
They can do one.

I'm going to have a word.
I am.
No, I'm going to.
I am.
I'm going to go absolutely mental about this.
Totally off my nut.
I'm stressing, mate.
Stressing big time.
I'm doing it.
Back me up, lads.
Here we go.
It's going to kick right off.

'Pardon me, so sorry
but I believe that these are our seats?
Perhaps you have the wrong row?
Oh, no issue at all!
Sorry to make you move.
Sorry.
Probably my fault.
Oh, thank you so much.
Again, so sorry.
Have an absolutely spectacular evening.'

Oh my gosh, lads
I was so savage
did you hear?
I destroyed them.
Such premium-grade banter, lads.

I hope Giles is OK.
Has anyone text him?
He's at home tucked up in bed
reading the new one by Murakami?
He's on a journey of postmodern magical realism
in the original Japanese?
LOL, what a banter merchant
absolute Bantersaurus Rex.

Alright lads, alright lads, settle down yeah?
Ballet's about to start.
Here. We. Go.
Three. Two. One.
Ballet.

Oh my gosh, lads, yeah
oh my gosh, she is well fit
literally
you obviously have to be in peak physical condition
to be principal dancer for the Bolshoi
and, mate, her Arabesque penchée is so on point!

En pointe, on point – yeah, get it, lads?
Boom! I tell you, she would totally get it from me:
she will totally get a standing ovation
from me at the end of the show
for the grace of her soubresaut alone.
Can you handle this spicy banter, lads?
Can you?

Ah, lads
lads
it's been a top night out
absolutely wicked
loads of laughs, top bantz
I feel off my face on this art
so mashed on culture
but listen, lads
I'd better be heading home
got an early start tomorrow:

I'm taking the little ones
to toddler yoga.

It's going to be
absolutely
fucking
mental.

SATURDAY/SUNDAY

Saturday pub:
a beery, bleary cheeriness.

Sunday bed:
a dreary, weary oh-dear-iness.

NOT CRICKET

Grass cut
neat trim
some men
fielding.

Gentlemen
willow leather
grey clouds
English weather.

No sun?
Chance of rain?
Who cares?
Let's play.

Gather pace
throw toss
backspin
runs lost.

Tap tap tap tap
see ball
swing bat
great thwack

run run
run run
hear cry:
'Howzat?'

Crowd shouts
'Not out!'
False alarm
raise arm.

Stop play
time for tea
get stung
by a bee.

Fast bowler
full toss
ball to groin
wore a box.

Still bruised
bad news
retire injured
can't have children…

Swing, miss
bit miffed
a duck
get pissed.

Hit for six
played for four
run for one
try one more.

Push for two
yes – no!
Get back!
Too slow.

Caught short
scored nought
throw bat.
Umpire says
'None of that.'

Get fined
don't mind
get the yips
forced to quit.

Red-faced
disgraced
turn to booze
front-page news.

Downward spiral
something viral
depression
silence
violence
life of crime
do some time.

Day release
see police
they can stick it.

Their car?
I brick it.
Went too far
sticky wicket.

This life?

It's just
not cricket.

CHRISTMAS OFFICE EXIT STRATEGY

Allow that eager end-of-year energy
to build up inside you
your professional demeanour slipping
a little.

Become barely-contained anticipation
a human advent calendar
for four weeks
counting down the days till you finish work
every day announcing
obnoxiously loudly
just how long is left
until you scream Noddy Holder style:
'IT'S CHRIIIIIIIIIIIIIISTMAAAAAS!!!'

Drink a little eggnog – go on, it's nearly Christmas after all!
Add new event to the office's shared calendar:
CHRISTMAS ANNUAL LEAVE
SEE YA NEXT YEAR, SUCKERS!
Your colleagues who have already used their annual leave
or didn't book it in time
will appreciate your increasingly effervescent cheer.

Rewrite the entirety of your to-do list with:
eat (all the food)
drink (all the booze)
open (all the presents)
love (all the people).

Decorate your desk with so much stuff
that your keyboard is inaccessible:
a mini Christmas tree with the shiniest baubles
and radioactively bright fairy lights
so your colleagues have to shield their eyes
whenever they walk past
– as a bonus, they won't see you drinking eggnog.

Place a wreath over your monitor
and hang the mouse like mistletoe
as your productivity melts away
like layers of snow generated by the machine
you've hired to Christmasify the office.

Use words like 'Christmasify'
at every available opportunity.

Drink more eggnog and put on that Christmas jumper
you tell everyone is meant to be ironic
but it is not really ironic
because you secretly love it, actually.

DO NOT WATCH *LOVE ACTUALLY*
UNDER ANY CIRCUMSTANCES.

Do not underestimate the power of Secret Santa
to send passive-aggressive messages to your colleagues:
Mark: your haircut has looked terrible for the past six months.
Aliyah: no one cares about every detail
of your very mundane weekend.
Mo: you don't have to type so loudly
to prove that you're working.
Yvonne: your homemade food offends my nostrils every day.
Terry: your jokes and comments are actually sexist.

Turn on your 'out of office' autoreply
tip your in-tray into the bin
shred whatever filing you have left to do
turn expense receipts into wrapping paper
make up spurious conclusions to your outstanding reports
shut down your computer by pouring eggnog
into the USB ports.

Remember that it is still early November
but that's basically Christmas, right?
And you're out of here soon.

A SHAPE POEM

This is a poem-shaped shape poem
with some really very long lines that go on for a lot longer
than you might expect and some much, much shorter ones
that
don't.

Sometimes it's hard to fit the thing
you want to say
into the right shape –
the words are all there
but they're messy
end up all over the place
don't look like anything at all
certainly not like a poem.

There is no shape to an insult
or an apology
a compliment
or a secret
no outline that can contain happiness
or anger
joy
or grief.

So what that you wrote a poem in the shape of a heart?
That doesn't mean your poem is more loving
because you fit your words into a certain shape.

Hearts don't look like that anyway
simple lines and curves
they are unformatted
messy and irregular;
each one is different
following no fixed pattern
or standard template.

They are folds of muscle
around emptying and filling space
continuous with the body
arteries stretching away to capillaries
lifelines of blood.

Hearts are constantly in motion
alive
so do not pin your heart to the page
stop it beating to help shape a poem –
don't fill your heart with words.

Fill your words with heart:
let them skip beats
and be unsure about what exactly they're trying to tell you –
your heart flutters and palpates
in a tumble of half-sentences anyway.

Stops
and
starts

like line-broken thoughts
begun and left
unfinished.

Your heart makes mistakes
disregards the edges of people
jumps into our mouths
where words go to die
trail off…

incomplete.

Love is not a shape poem
meaning and form in harmony
you can't always write inside the lines
so you shouldn't
even
try.

ACKNOWLEDGEMENTS

With thanks: to my friends who offered feedback on the book, come to my shows, and keep me grounded; to my fellow spoken word professionals – you are a source of inspiration and support; to my parents for their constant care and love; to all the organisations I work with – and enable me to say that poetry is my job; and to the crew at Burning Eye Books for their patience, professionalism, and sheer hard work in making this sort of thing happen.

Lightning Source UK Ltd.
Milton Keynes UK
UKHW041634061219
354840UK00006B/426/P